Contested Decisions

Priority setting in the NHS

Chris Ham and Shirley McIver

Published by
King's Fund Publishing
11–13 Cavendish Square
London W1M 0AN

First published 2000

ISBN 1 85717 418 6

A CIP catalogue record for this book is available from the British Library

Available from:
King's Fund Bookshop
11–13 Cavendish Square
London
W1M 0AN
Tel: 020 7307 2591
Fax: 020 7307 2801

Printed and bound in Great Britain

Cover illustration by Minuche Mazumdar Farrar

Contents

Acknowledgements

Thanks are due to the King's Fund, who supported the research on which this book is based, and to all those who were interviewed during the research and allowed us access to papers and files. We would also like to thank Anne van der Salm and Jackie Francis at the Health Services Management Centre for their secretarial and administrative support.

Chapter 1

Introduction

Priority setting in the NHS is not new but it is assuming increasing significance. Although the NHS Executive publishes annual guidance on planning and priorities, the main responsibility for making decisions about which services are given priority and whether or not some types of treatment should be funded rests at a local level.

A recent working party on priority setting in the NHS recommended that further work should be carried out to establish the most effective approaches to making these decisions (Academy of Royal Medical Colleges *et al*. 1997). One way of contributing to this work is to examine how priority setting is currently carried out.

The working party's report identified three levels at which priorities in the NHS are set:

- **macro** decisions are made by governments and determine the level of resources devoted to health and the amount that each health authority receives

- **meso** decisions are made by health authorities and GP fundholding practices (or the newly established primary care groups) and relate to the amount of money that they assign to each programme or speciality on behalf of their residents

- **micro** decisions are made by health professionals and determine which individuals receive or are referred to specific services within the resources allocated as a consequence of meso decision-making.

Although the levels can be separated analytically, they are clearly inter-related and decisions made at one level will have an impact on those made at others.

There has been research on:

- setting priorities in health authorities (Klein, Day and Redmayne, 1996; Ham, Honigsbaum and Thompson, 1993)

- involving the public (Bowie, Richardson and Sykes, 1995; McIver, 1998; Lenaghan, New and Mitchell, 1996)

- using an ethical framework (Crisp, Hope and Ebbs, 1996)

- applying health economics (Mooney *et al.* 1992).

By comparison, there has been little work on the way in which decisions made at different levels interact. The translation of decisions set at the meso level into action at the micro level is likely to be of particular interest because historically micro level decisions have been the responsibility of clinicians.

Clinicians working in trusts and general practitioners are now expected to work with health authorities to agree more explicit ways of making choices about who will or will not receive particular treatments. In doing so, they may well find that ethical requirements to prescribe the best care for individual patients brings them into conflict with those whose job it is to decide the most cost effective use of resources across a community or population. With GPs increasingly involved in commissioning services, there is the potential for conflict between their roles as agents and advocates for individual patients on the one hand, and as commissioners of services to improve the health of a community on the other.

The challenges involved in setting priorities at the meso and micro levels may be studied by examining examples where the funding of a treatment was questioned or refused. Child B was one such example and an earlier analysis examined this case in detail, drawing out the implications for patients, managers and professionals and making recommendations about how decisions of this kind might be handled in future (Ham and Pickard, 1998). This book is based on research into five further cases. It aims to assess whether the lessons to emerge from the experience of Child B have wider relevance and application.

Due to the sensitive nature of the subject matter, these cases were chosen from among health authorities that were willing to have their decisions subjected to scrutiny. The point of the research was not to critically appraise decisions but to compare experiences and learn from them about the way in which priorities are set by health authorities and applied at the level of the individual patient. The information will be of particular interest to the new primary care groups, which lack experience in this area.

The cases were identified following approaches made to regional directors of public health in the eight English regions. These approaches were supplemented with information gathered from health authorities involved in a learning network on priority setting co-ordinated by the Health Services Management Centre at the University of Birmingham. Five health authorities that had been involved in contested treatment decisions were contacted to establish whether they were willing to take part in the study.

The chief executive or director of public health in each health authority was interviewed using a checklist of questions employed in previous research into the Child B case. Each interview, which took approximately 90 minutes, was recorded and the tape transcribed by the interviewer. Additional documents, such as court transcripts and health authority policies and procedures, were collected where available, and a small number of additional interviews were carried out to supplement the data gathered from health authorities.

No patients or families were interviewed. This followed advice that it might further damage relationships between patients and families and the health authorities concerned and re-open experiences that had caused pain or distress. The descriptions of the cases in this book have been checked with the health authorities concerned for accuracy.

This book is organised as follows:

- **Case studies** describe the five cases and explain how they were handled

- **Analysis** examines the roles of health authorities, clinicians, patients, the courts, the media and the Department of Health

- **Strengthening decision-making** relates the findings to the wider debate about priority setting and indicates how decision-making might be improved.

Chapter 2

Case studies

The Child B case provided a stimulus for this research but the aim was to examine a range of examples where health authority decisions about whether or not to fund treatment had been controversial. In fact, only one of the five cases – Case 1 – had obvious similarities to that of Child B. This involved a four-year-old child with a malignant brain tumour whose parents travelled to the USA for treatment. The other four cases were quite different:

- **Case 2** involved a middle-aged woman with advanced ovarian cancer whose clinician wanted to prescribe a new drug called Taxol

- **Case 3** concerned a patient being treated for gender reorientation whose psychiatrist recommended gender reassignment surgery

- **Case 4** involved a young man with multiple sclerosis whose clinician wanted to prescribe a new drug called beta-interferon

- **Case 5** concerned an eight-year-old child with haemophilia who developed antibodies to the factor VIII treatment he was receiving and whose doctor recommended a high dose factor VIII treatment to reduce the tolerance to the drug.

Case 1

Key points

- Four-year-old child with malignant brain tumour.

- UK specialist advised no curative treatment available.

- Child's parents referred themselves to a specialist in the USA who claimed he could operate with a 20 per cent chance of success.

- Local MP helped family to visit the USA and requested NHS funding.

- Health authority (HA) found itself thrust into the glare of publicity over funding.

- HA refused to fund US treatment.

- Local public support paid for treatment.

- Child died on return to UK after approximately four months.

Outline of events

This case arose in 1995 and involved a four-year-old child (Child X) who was suffering from a malignant brain tumour. The child had surgery, which removed part of the tumour, followed by chemotherapy. A further operation was carried out to remove a recurrence of the tumour and a course of radiotherapy was given. Following the treatment there were several re-admissions to hospital for symptoms and complications. The specialist responsible for Child X advised that no further curative treatment was recommended because the chances of benefit from an operation would be outweighed by the risks. A second opinion confirmed this.

The child's parents did not accept the advice they received and referred themselves to a specialist in the USA who offered surgery followed by intensive chemotherapy and bone marrow transplant. The parents also contacted their local MP for help, saying that they wanted to fly out to the USA as soon as possible and needed practical assistance. As the MP commented during an interview:

The parents had been offered this opportunity. They wanted to take it and the indication was that come hell or high water they were going to go through with it. Therefore my job was to try and help them. Time was of the absolute essence and so there wasn't much thinking time available. I pulled out all the stops to get them the visas and the other things they needed and worked with the British Embassy in Washington.

The parents asked the MP if he could find out whether the NHS would fund the treatment in the USA. The MP contacted the office of the Secretary of State who referred the matter to the NHS Executive's Corporate Affairs Intelligence Unit. The MP also approached the local health authority and requested funding for the child's treatment. The same evening he appeared on the local TV news and made the following points:

- UK specialists were unable to help (Child X) further and without treatment she would die

- a US specialist had agreed to treat the child

- the MP had asked the local health authority to consider funding the treatment

- the MP recognised that UK medical considerations would need to be balanced with the understandable but more emotive wishes of the parents

- a public appeal had been launched.

The health authority immediately found itself under pressure to make a decision quickly. As the Director of Public Health explained:

> *It all came upon us rather fast because we didn't know about it until after the press had announced through the MP that the child was flying to America ... There wasn't any organised period for calm reflection.*

The fact that the MP had contacted the Department of Health, and the case received publicity, meant that the government became involved. The Chief Executive of the health authority was on holiday when the case arose and the Director of Public Health received phone calls from the office of the Secretary of State requesting information. Based on the information initially available, the Director of Public Health thought at first that the health authority should fund the treatment. As he explained:

> *... it is very difficult for a health authority to say 'no' to an individual patient and particularly a child when a consultant, albeit one from another country, has recommended a particular treatment.*

When requests are made to fund overseas treatment, a health authority has to obtain approval from the Department of Health. A submission was prepared, making a case that rested on the following points:

- while the conduct of other health authorities was an important point of reference, each case deserved individual consideration

- the voice of the patient, represented by the parents, needed to be heard as strongly as medical opinion

- the treatment was affordable to the health authority and had it been the subject of an extra-contractual funding request within the internal market the health authority would have approved it

- the health authority is required to consider international opportunity and professional opinion (even when in contrast with UK professional opinion) when focused on a particular member of its resident population. The health authority was unaware of any national policy to the contrary.

This letter was never sent because within the space of a few days the Director of Public Health changed his mind and made a different recommendation to the health authority. This was as a result of the information and advice he received from medical experts and the NHS Executive.

The Director of Public Health contacted the specialists involved in the case and they both advised that the chances of benefit from the procedure were outweighed by the risks. National experts in neurosurgery and chemotherapy were involved, leading to a health authority document summarising the medical information, which stated:

> There clearly is a requirement for the tumour to be removed completely, whereas in [Child X's] case this was not done at the initial operation, presumably because other structures would have been damaged, and the tumour has regrown several times. The tumour does not appear to be responsive to the chemotherapy and radiotherapy already given and it is doubtful therefore whether there will be a response to further therapy.

The other experts consulted also advised that the treatment proposed by the US specialist was available in the UK, in some cases attracting referrals from overseas, including the USA.

The NHS Executive's Medical Director advised that the responsibility for making the decision lay with the health authority and that the decision-making process should be clearly structured. In a letter to the Director of Public Health, he advised:

Nationally, we are concerned that the public can be assured that there is a clear process for considering cases of this kind, founded on values and principles which have been shared with the public, and which your Authority would be prepared to see applied in other cases.

He enquired whether the health authority had established any values and principles that could be used and this prompted it to refer to a paper that it had published the previous year entitled a *Framework for a Health Strategy.*

The Medical Director also clarified the criteria the Department of Health normally applied to requests for funding for treatment overseas and which were being developed into national guidelines. The main criteria for approval were:

- that the condition involved was of a serious nature

- that suitable treatment was not available within the UK

- that the treatment was well-established

- that there was a probability of significant benefit to the patient.

In the letter he also drew attention to relevant aspects of the guidance on extra-contractual referrals (ECRs), including the very limited grounds on which an ECR could be refused:

... the referral is not justified on clinical grounds. In making such judgements the DHA would be expected to ensure that it takes appropriate clinical advice. This would include instances where such clinical advice has led to the development and agreement of clear referral protocols and the threshold has not been met.

He also pointed out that the guidance was clear on patient self-referrals which:

... should be considered in the same way as those resulting from referral by a GP or other clinicians.

In the light of the information and advice received, the Director of Public Health recommended that the treatment should not be funded. In presenting his argument to the Board, he used the authority's framework of values. The following is a summary of points made:

Appropriateness

There is clear and consistent advice from Child X's clinicians, who are leading experts in their field, that at this stage there is no curative treatment available; that the aim of further treatment should be to control symptoms; and that all active treatment is inappropriate because it carries significant risks with the prospect of only temporary respite.

Effectiveness

The treatment offered by the US specialist is available in the UK. The difference is that the US specialist is willing to perform the treatment whilst doctors in this country are not. No information is available on the long-term follow-up and outcome of his patients. There is no evidence that surgery and chemotherapy at this stage of the disease will be effective.

Responsiveness

The health authority should take into account the views of (Child X's) parents who have expressed their wishes through their actions and via their MP. Treatment in the USA is also supported by a large number of the general public who have given generously to the appeal that has been launched. There is a general feeling that 'all that can be done should be done'. In this case however the patient is a child who is too young to express a view. In making their decision, the health authority should act above all in what they see as the best interests of the child.

Equity

As a responsible funding body the health authority must weigh up the competing needs of the individual case with the needs of the population as a whole. Given the lack of benefit expected from the specific treatment, and the potential dangers to the child, the cost of lost opportunity for others that the expenditure would signify must be taken into account.

Efficiency

The treatment costs, estimated at £100,000, are significant but are not in themselves a critical factor. Already this year expenditure of greater sums has been agreed on treatment of individuals on a number of occasions where appropriate treatment was shown to be effective.

The Director of Public Health's advice to the health authority also made two other points:

- the wider context of the child's ongoing care should be taken into consideration and health care would be needed on the child's return from the USA

- the effect of the decision on other patients in similar situations should be considered and any support encouraging unrealistic expectation and continuation of inappropriate treatment should be discouraged.

The issue was taken to a health authority board meeting where it was agreed that the treatment in the USA should not be funded on the grounds that it was inappropriate, not effective, and not in the best interests of the child. The child eventually received the treatment in the USA funded by local public support. She returned home and died approximately four months after the operation.

Analysis of events

An important feature of this case was that the parents did not accept the prognosis and recommendations for care offered by the NHS specialists treating their child. The Director of Public Health said that there was some indication that the relationship had broken down before the final prognosis:

> The consultants had warned in their notes that the father had not accepted their advice and was likely to seek alternative treatments and they regretted that that might happen. I think there is an issue about the personal relationship between the doctors and the parents in the case. Clearly the doctors were right but the parents didn't accept their advice and sought alternative treatment.

The parents did not meet anyone from the health authority because the request for funding was made after they had left for the USA. The parents' impression that the NHS had failed their child was therefore gained before the health authority became involved. The refusal to fund merely reinforced an earlier belief that treatment was being refused on the grounds of cost. The MP recalled the family's perception of the situation in the following way:

> … into this equation is injected a belief from an American consultant that there is treatment available at a cost in America, that is not available or being made available in this country. Overlaid on that is the insinuation that this is simply a question of cost and that in fact if we were prepared to shell out whatever it cost then the job could be done in this country, and should be done.

The MP emphasised that the parents wanted to do all they could for their child. The treatment they had been offered, which was to control the symptoms rather than actively seek to cure the condition, did not seem to fulfil this objective.

Publicity was mainly of a local nature, although a national Sunday newspaper took enough interest in the case to report that they had approached the surgeon concerned who, as a result, had agreed to carry out the operation free of charge. Much of the publicity was descriptive in nature and there was less comment and criticism of the health authority than expected by the Director of Public Health. As he explained:

> We were surprised in a way that this case didn't draw more media attention but I think it was because it was a subsequent case to Child B. Partly also because by that time the family were in America.

There may also have been an element of doubt in the minds of those reporting the case over whether or not the parents were doing the right thing. In one of the reports carried in the national newspaper, the suffering of the child is clearly described. For example:

> As we near the scanning room she begins to sweat and shake. She waves her skinny arms around in small jerky movements. Her eyes frantically begin to roll around in her head as the doctor says: 'Just one last scan ...'. She begins to scream. 'Please mummy, daddy, no more.' I turn away because I cannot look at this kind of terror in the face of a child.

Despite this, the Director of Public Health felt that the vast majority of the public 'just accepted that the health authority were mean, bureaucratic and penny-pinching' and it would have been impossible to make a case in favour of the decision not to fund. He noted:

> The really interesting thing about the case is that although we believed that it was the right thing to do, I don't think we'd ever be successful in making the case somehow. Even in discussions with my own family there was disagreement. There is a view that if there is a chance, however small, you should take it, but that really wasn't backed up by the medical evidence.

An important feature of this case was conflict between the clinicians treating the child in the UK and the doctors in the USA contacted by the parents. The experts in different countries seemed to weigh the risks and benefits differently. In deciding whether or not it would be beneficial to carry out a further operation followed by chemotherapy and bone marrow transplant, the UK specialists considered the benefit of short-term remission at best was not worth the risk of injury and suffering to the child. The US consultant, on the other hand, led the parents to believe there was a 20 per cent chance of success. The health authority's report summarising the medical information available pointed out that the US specialist did not follow-up his patients and left much of the responsibility for the oncology treatment to the referring hospital. As a consequence:

> … it may therefore be difficult to establish or evaluate long term outcomes of patients treated by him.

As these comments indicate, there was a disagreement about the ethics of experimental procedures, and the conditions under which the NHS should fund them. As the MP pointed out:

> … people like the guy in America and similar ones in this country do have to have cases to work on if they are going to make any progress. [Child X] didn't live but it's not inconceivable that ten years down the road another child may live because of this child and four or five others in between and the knowledge gained from them. But are we in the business of funding that kind of research in that way?

Summary

- Child B was not an exceptional case – many aspects are repeated in Child X.

- Issues can, as here, descend on a health authority without warning forcing it to make decisions quickly.

- Expert advice and further information or guidance can result in a health authority changing its decision.

- Conflict in medical opinion between clinicians in the UK and the USA can be as difficult to resolve as that between clinicians in the UK.

- A values framework may be useful in helping a health authority to make a decision.

- When the clinician's values and views diverge from those of the parents (or patient) it can result in the family making their own decisions about what is the best treatment.

- There can be difficulty in establishing what is in the best interests of the child.

- There may be difficulty in establishing when the NHS should fund experimental procedures.

Case 2

Key points

- Middle-aged woman with advanced ovarian cancer.

- Cancer had gone into remission and returned three times.

- Consultant wanted to prescribe the drug Taxol.

- HA was asked informally if it would pay.

- HA refused, based on evidence of effectiveness.

- HA found itself an object of media criticism.

- Regional Director of Public Health suggested independent expert clinical advice.

- Independent expert recommended that the patient would benefit.

- HA agreed to fund Taxol treatment.

- Patient lived a further 18 months.

Outline of events

This case emerged in 1995 and involved a middle-aged woman who several years earlier had been diagnosed as having an ovarian cyst. Surgery confirmed advanced ovarian cancer. The patient was offered further treatment with chemotherapy. Following this treatment, she was well for five years but then the cancer returned. The patient was treated again with radiotherapy and chemotherapy.

The cancer went into remission but the patient relapsed two years later and was treated with an operation and chemotherapy, after which she achieved another remission. This lasted only a few months and she returned to her consultant for further treatment. He wanted to prescribe a new drug called Taxol but the health authority responsible for services in the hospital where the patient was being *treated* did not approve funding of the drug for this condition. The consultant then approached the health authority responsible for services in the area where the patient *lived*. He did this in an informal way, asking in a letter 'if we send you an extra-contractual referral of this kind, will you approve it?'. The health authority said it would not because, as the Director of Public Health explained:

We were at that stage quite deeply into negotiations with our main local oncology hospital and hadn't agreed the use of Taxol with them, so in terms of fairness we did not think we could say 'yes' to Taxol in this particular case.

The health authority's decision was based upon information gained from reading reviews of evidence of effectiveness. The Director of Public Health explained:

There was a review in the Drug and Therapeutics Bulletin *basically saying that this drug should not be used for ovarian cancer except under research conditions, and there was a review in the* Lancet *which said much the same. One awkward bit was that we also looked up the reference in the* British National Formulary *and at that stage our BNF, which was about four months old at the time we looked at it, didn't give ovarian cancer as an indication. What we didn't know was that there was a new edition in which it was given as an indication.*

Shortly afterwards and without warning, the health authority found itself the subject of complaint and criticism in the media. The consultant concerned had told the patient that he was going to ask her local health authority if it would fund the treatment and so when the refusal was given, she became angry at the health authority. The patient contacted the local press and they covered the story intensively. As the Director of Public Health recalled:

The next thing we got was a storm of media protest from this woman saying this is my last chance, you ought to pay for the drug, what are you going to do now? Basically we got swamped at that stage by press and I spent three days doing nothing but dealing with phone calls.

A further complication was establishing who was responsible for paying for the treatment. The patient's consultant asked her GP, who was a fundholder, whether his practice would sustain the cost of treatment, which was likely to be about £6000. The GP's view was that this was not a fundholding procedure and the practice would not purchase it.

Commenting on this, the Regional Director of Public Health noted:

When the case came up, it sprang on people – a kind of sideways attack. There was confusion over whether the GP or health authority would pay.

The press was particularly concerned to find out whether the cost of the drug was the reason funding had been refused. The health authority explained the decision was based on medical evidence but this was not completely convincing because some health authorities were funding Taxol and others were not. In a background paper for members of the health authority, the Director of Public Health stated:

… I had calls, some repeated, from newspapers, news agencies, radio and television. All essentially asked the same questions: had the decision been made on the grounds of cost – to which I said no – and if not why – clinical effectiveness. Some of the callers had spoken to hospitals which were using Taxol, to which I replied that I

knew of others who did not, and of other Authorities who did not fund it.

The health authority also received calls from the regional health authority, asking for briefings for the NHS Executive and for ministers.

When it became clear to the Director of Public Health that 'we needed a better explanation', he spoke to the Regional Director of Public Health who suggested that a second opinion should be sought. As the Regional Director of Public Health explained:

> *I was concerned whether if the case was taken to judicial review then the health authority would be asked what advice it had taken, so I suggested they needed to take some advice. As it was a cancer case and I was in the early stages of implementing Calman, I knew someone who could give an expert opinion. It took some of the steam out of the situation. Instead of the patient, the GP and the health authority communicating by press release as was happening, a face-to-face discussion with the patient was needed. She needed to feel that someone cared about her.*

In recommending that the patient see an independent expert, the Regional Director of Public Health provided a solution to two problems. The first was the health authority's need for an independent opinion to help it make a decision. The independent expert's view after seeing the patient enabled a decision to be made which took into account the individual patient, rather than one based at the level of all patients in that particular category. It was also potentially a way through the dilemma that the clinical evidence suggested the drug should only be used as part of a trial. The expert consulted was doing research in this area and the Regional Director of Public Health hoped the patient would be eligible for one of his trials. The second problem was the importance of finding a way to restore the patient's faith in the NHS. The patient needed something which would reassure her that the NHS was concerned about her welfare, rather than a bureaucracy making decisions based upon abstract principles, such as cost effectiveness and efficiency.

The oncology expert found he needed to explain to the patient why she had not been given the Taxol treatment automatically, in order to reassure her that she had not been treated unjustly. He did this by explaining in some detail the information he had amassed through clinical experience. He described how he did this:

> *I explained carefully and at great length the meaning and implication of the 20 per cent response rate we can expect using Paclitaxel in this context … I told her that out of 30 patients I'd treated with Taxol for recurrent ovarian cancer who had been previously treated with Taxol, only six or seven had responded, and all of these bar one were relatively short-lived with the disease progressing for worse within a month. I went on to explain that most clinicians thought the benefits were marginal … I was defusing her anger at her feeling that she had been deprived of treatment by explaining how we had been using Taxol, and she accepted this I think.*

The oncologist was able to recommend that she be prescribed Taxol. The main reason hinged on the fact that in a letter explaining why the health authority had declined to authorise the use of the drug, the Director of Public Health had given the reason as due to concerns about 'the use of a relatively new and toxic drug from which any benefit in quality of life or survival is still in doubt'. The issues therefore appeared to be:

● newness

● toxicity

● whether there would be any benefit to quality of life.

The consultant was able to answer all three challenges. He explained that although the licence was new, it had been used in clinical trials for ten years. As far as benefit to quality of life was concerned, he argued that this depended on the likely response of the patient to the treatment. He looked at:

- whether the cancer was one which responded to treatment

- what condition the patient was in.

His assessment of the patient led him to argue:

> I thought she would respond to treatment, and she was fairly well, so the cost–benefit ratio was good. If she had been insured for private medicine I would have given her Taxol, so I was prepared to treat her. I thought it was worthwhile.

This meant that:

> The only issue therefore was the toxicity. That made it easy for me. This wasn't an issue because Taxol is not a terribly toxic drug. It has few side effects.

He discussed with the patient the clinical trials for which she might be eligible but he considered that she should not be included because they were using a combination of drugs and this would not suit her for various reasons. They agreed that she would have two cycles of Taxol treatment to see if she responded, and then further treatment if she did.

The health authority found the oncologist's second opinion useful in two ways:

- he said there were factors which would make the patient's life expectancy better than others

- he said the patient could have a course of two treatments followed by tests and if these proved to be encouraging, she could have the next two treatments. In this way some control was brought to the process and it was not an open-ended commitment.

In the light of the second opinion, the health authority agreed to fund the treatment. The patient survived for a further 18 months, which was considerably longer than expected. In the event the health authority funded eight courses of therapy comprising four courses of two cycles each.

Analysis of events

An important aspect of this case is that the consultant told the patient that he wanted to prescribe her Taxol. Indeed, she may even have been encouraged to see it as her only hope of survival. In a background summary document for members of the health authority, the Director of Public Health remarked:

> … we learnt through informal channels that [patient's initials] had been told by the consultant that he wanted to use the drug as it was her 'last chance', but that [the health authority] would not pay for it.

From the patient's point of view, the health authority was preventing her from obtaining the treatment she needed. In retrospect the Director of Public Health considered that it might have been better to arrange to speak directly with the patient. Letters did not seem effective because he did write to her explaining what the health authority was doing, and asking her to contact him if she had any questions or wanted to discuss things further, but he did not receive a reply. Also it did not seem to be enough to rely on the patient's GP to explain what was happening. As the Director of Public Health noted:

> The GP did talk to the woman, but this was the point I realised I couldn't actually assume I could give a message to another doctor or a consultant and assume that it would go through automatically. I

should actually have been much more up front and maybe gone and talked to her myself personally.

In fact the Director of Public Health considered the experience had taught the health authority an important lesson about communication. There was a tendency to concentrate on the issue and the process of reaching a decision rather than on communication. Normal communication channels and routes were relied upon but the high profile and controversial nature of the decision meant that it more closely resembled an emergency situation. And in refusing to fund treatment, the health authority was sharing in clinical decision-making with the patient's GP and consultant. This meant that the health authority had a responsibility to the patient to explain why it had made a decision and to become involved in trying to find alternatives acceptable to the patient.

The picture that the patient saw and which was reproduced in the local press was a black and white one in which the patient had been prescribed a drug which she needed and the 'bureaucratic' health authority had refused to fund it because there were insufficient resources available. As the Director of Public Health described it:

... 60-year-old sweet grey-haired grandmother is being refused treatment by the heartless health authority.

This picture was reinforced by confusion over who would fund the treatment, with the trust consultants recommending treatment without having first obtained an agreement on who would fund it, and the GPs involved passing responsibility to the health authority. This confusion contributed to the emphasis in the media on cost rather than the uncertainty about clinical appropriateness, even though from the health authority's point of view, the question of whether or not the drug was considered effective in the treatment of late stage ovarian cancer was crucial.

The clinical uncertainty may also have been masked by a press release, issued by the drug company which manufactures Taxol, a few days after the case received publicity. On 24 May 1995, Bristol–Myers Squibb Pharmaceuticals Limited issued a press release which announced a 'breakthrough' in treatment for ovarian cancer, stating:

> *Women with advanced ovarian cancer can extend their average survival time by 50 per cent with initial use of combination chemotherapy with the new drug Taxol (Paclitaxel) according to results of a US clinical study, revealed today.*

It appeared that clinical uncertainty in the UK about whether or not Taxol was effective in the treatment of advanced ovarian cancer was not sufficiently explained to the patient until several weeks had passed and she saw the specialist who was called in to provide a second opinion. He recounted how he had to explain the risks, benefits and probable outcomes of treatment in some detail before the patient's anger at being 'refused treatment' had subsided. This included an explanation that:

> *most clinicians practising in the UK at present would see the benefits of treatment as relatively marginal and I specifically referred to the poor duration of response seen in earlier clinical trials here.*

The specialist who acted as an independent expert therefore fulfilled a very important role in applying the clinical evidence to the individual case. His detailed knowledge of the drug and others used in the treatment of ovarian cancer enabled him to weigh up its usefulness in this particular case. He then suggested a framework that enabled the drug to be administered in a controlled way so that treatment could be stopped when it was no longer effective.

This specialist had a further important and ultimately beneficial influence. The framework within which the drug was to be administered required that the trust's consultants work with the health authority in order to provide the information needed to make a decision whether or not to continue treatment. As the Director of Public Health explained, this proved difficult at first but eventually worked very well:

> It still didn't go that smoothly, basically because initially at least we had real difficulties getting the information we wanted from the trust. They would wait until the very last minute and then we'd get a letter from them saying 'we want to bring her in and treat her tomorrow, will you approve an ECR?' and we had to be quite blunt in writing back and say ' no, we said we'd only approve an ECR when we were given certain monitoring information which we haven't received. Send us that information and we'll think about it'. But it got better. By the end of the treatment it was going pretty smoothly and subsequently to that we've had two patients in a similar situation and in these cases I've had very thorough letters from the consultant in [name of hospital] saying 'here are the details of the patient, these are the investigations I have carried out, I think two courses of treatment are warranted, will you approve that and I will write to you again' and so on. Clearly the consultant learned how to keep us happy. On that basis we have approved a couple of treatments subsequently.

As a result of his experience with the case, the Director of Public Health made suggestions for future health authority policy on handling refusals to fund extra-contractual referrals. These included:

- inform the patient of the decision and reasons behind it as early as possible

- explore other options as early as possible with the GP and consultant

- use a wide range of information sources, such as the Regional Director of Public Health and university departments

- in the event of media pressure, share responsibilities so that one person deals with enquiries while another collects information

- ensure good internal communication

- provide advanced press relations training to staff who may be involved.

The case was discussed within the region concerned at a meeting of regional directors of public health, where it was decided to develop good practice guidelines on handling difficult ECRs. The guidelines included advice on:

- recognising a difficult ECR, such as the features that may make a decision complex

- conducting the process of decision-making

- handling communication with others

- dealing with press enquiries.

The guidelines incorporated what the health authority had learned from the case including the importance of speaking or writing to people personally rather than relying on messages through others, keeping the patient informed, documenting sources of information and keeping copies of all communication, considering alternatives to the proposed therapy and asking for a second opinion.

Summary

- When, as here, a patient is recommended a drug by a specialist and the health authority refuses to fund it, the patient may feel aggrieved.

- In circumstances such as these, it is difficult to avoid becoming clinically involved with the patient and this brings additional responsibilities.

- A health authority can suddenly find itself in the middle of a media storm with no warning (as in the case of Child X).

- Expert advice can result in a health authority changing its decision.

- An expert adviser can play a crucial role in resolving difficult decisions and defusing controversy.

- Effective communications, both internal and external, are extremely important in ensuring that a health authority receives fair and accurate media coverage and that patients understand the reasons for decisions.

Case 3

Key points

- Patient being treated for gender reorientation.

- Several requests made by psychiatrists and local MP to HA for funding for surgery over four years.

- HA refused request on grounds that this treatment was excluded from funding.

- Application for judicial review on her behalf received by HA.

- HA took counsel's advice and found their policy not to fund had weaknesses.

- HA examined its policy and sought advice from others.

- HA decided to amend its policy to enable greater consideration of individual cases.

- If patient gets through agreed protocol then surgery will be funded.

Outline of events

This case involved a patient who was being treated for gender reorientation. Her psychiatrist wrote to the health authority in 1993 asking for permission to refer her to a surgeon. After discussing the case with the Director of Public Health, the Chief Executive replied indicating that the health authority had decided the previous year that certain types of treatment were not approved within the ECR process and gender reassignment surgery was one of them. This was because treatments of 'a controversial nature' were excluded. As the Chief Executive explained:

So the policy we were following was that for gender reorientation problems we supported counselling and hormone therapy but we did not support surgery on the basis that in priority-setting terms there have always been higher priorities.

The following year the health authority received a letter from a local MP who had been visited by the patient. In the letter, he said he was:

very concerned if [patient's initial] is unable to obtain treatment simply because of where she happens to live.

The Chief Executive replied that the patient might wish to consider asking her GP to refer her to the local psychiatric service. Shortly afterwards the Chief Executive received a letter from a local psychiatrist requesting an operation for the patient as:

without the operation I fear she is at great risk of suicide, unable to live in the 'halfway' situation of limbo she is currently in.

A letter was sent to the psychiatrist reiterating the health authority's position that it did not approve funding for gender reassignment operations. Further letters between the health authority, the MP and the psychiatrist followed until in 1996 the health authority received a solicitor's letter stating that they had advised the patient to apply for a judicial review of the decision and that 'leave has already been granted in two similar cases against health authorities.' The health authority duly received an application for judicial review on her behalf. This questioned the policy and asked a number of questions, including:

- was the health authority employing a blanket ban and not taking into account the full circumstances of the individual?

- was its process rational in that it funded part of the treatment but not surgery?

- was it discriminating against a category of person?

The health authority took counsel's advice and to its surprise found that its policy had a number of weaknesses. As the Chief Executive explained:

> We thought we'd made a rational priority-setting judgement that this kind of surgery was low priority compared with mental health development and so on and therefore we were completely justified in saying that normally we would give this low priority. The initial reaction was to assume that we could challenge the judicial review on the basis that in the end we've got to balance the books and some things get funded and some don't. Looking at counsel's advice there were weaknesses in our policies that we hadn't appreciated ...

These weaknesses were identified as follows:

- it looked as though the health authority had a blanket ban on gender reassignment surgery even though it could cite a number of other low priority areas such as *in vitro* fertilisation (IVF) and experimental treatment where it had looked at individual cases and approved treatment

- there was a question about what the term 'controversial' meant: did it mean medically controversial (which might be acceptable) or socially controversial (which might be challenged)?

- was it being rational in limiting gender reorientation when it is 75 per cent successful compared with IVF which is less successful?

The possibility of a judicial review stimulated the health authority to think more carefully about how it was making priority-setting decisions. As the Chief Executive pointed out:

The overall issues are how the health authority goes through a priority-setting process which is defensible publicly and in court. At the heart of this is the distinction between types of treatment and the treatment of individual patients.

In other words, what matters is making sure that the policy explains how individual patients can be fitted within the general policy framework in a way which is demonstrably rational and fair. Weaknesses in the health authority's approach were noted by their legal advisers, who pointed out:

*I appreciate that the authority has considered from time to time whether or not to **change** the policy: but there is no indication at all that it has ever considered whether to **depart** from that policy in the light of [the patient's] individual circumstances.*

The health authority's use of language was also found to be a problem. The Chief Executive expanded on this point:

... it's this term which we use 'controversial', which is whether something should be part of the NHS service or not and then its relative priority against other parts of the NHS – how far gender reorientation is cosmetic. ... I think it's a problem about the slack use of language. We were clear by 'controversial' we meant not necessarily generally regarded as core NHS business, which I suppose is a mixture of the medical debate about the efficacy of the procedure but also the question about relative priority. Clearly the words we used were not sharp enough.

In carrying out this examination of the way it made decisions about what it should and should not fund and how this was applied in individual cases, the health authority found that it was probably not treating those who requested gender reassignment surgery in the same way as those who requested IVF or other low priority treatments. As the Chief Executive explained:

We had in the light of individual circumstances agreed IVF treatment beyond our very limited amount each year – we had agreed to experimental treatment which would normally not be funded, on the basis that the case being put was so strong. So I suppose a similar situation here might have been if the consultant or consultant psychiatrist was saying 'waive your normal reluctance because, say, the psychiatric treatment she needed was costing more than the surgery would have been', or if her individual circumstances had been pressed upon us like they had been for some IVF treatment … We didn't explore the individual circumstances in this case, so there was a gap on our side…We certainly hadn't got a routine policy about looking at the individual circumstances, as we had for IVF.

During the examination of its gender reorientation policy, a consultant in public health medicine at the health authority carried out research to find out how other health authorities handled the issue. The Chief Executive said he decided to get the public health department to do this because:

There was the question of equity … if we had found we were the only ones not funding it, that would have been unfair.

The health authority found that another health authority had a particularly well-developed policy, which used a protocol adopted by a specialist gender identity clinic at Charing Cross Hospital. The Chief Executive thought that:

In the end it was the question of whether for some patients surgery was the only treatment that would resolve their whole mental health problem. The only way that their overall mental health would be improved. The Charing Cross Protocol was able to demonstrate that there would be health gain in the end. Excluding people from treatment that they would benefit from – that's an ethical issue.

There was also a cost effectiveness argument. As he put it:

If the costs of supporting someone with mental health problems in a lifetime are likely to be more than the costs of surgery then it is hardly rational to condemn someone to a lifetime of possibly unemployment or inability to get work and having psychiatric support.

The threat of judicial review also encouraged the health authority to look in much more detail at the evidence around gender reorientation surgery. In carrying this out it identified experts who were able to provide advice which enabled it to make its decision-making process more sophisticated. The health authority decided to refer patients who requested gender reorientation to the Charing Cross Clinic and if they successfully complied with their protocol, surgery would be funded. As the Chief Executive saw it:

I am persuaded that if someone gets through the Charing Cross Protocol, particularly living as the other sex, their future support from the NHS would be better through surgery than through psychiatric support. It would be a better use of money than psychiatric support. Some people who request gender reorientation have also got a psychiatric illness which the gender reorientation wouldn't solve, so I think it's actually important to rely on tertiary advice about whether the surgery would help the individual to function in society.

The patient was referred to the Charing Cross Clinic and surgery will be funded if she meets the criteria outlined in the protocol.

Analysis of events

In this case the relationship between the health authority and the patient was a slow burning fuse. The Chief Executive of the health authority received a letter from the patient's consultant requesting permission for a referral to a surgeon three years before he received notification of an intended judicial review. From the patient's point of view the gender reassignment surgery was a necessary part of the treatment she was receiving. This was made clear in the application for judicial review, which stated that the patient had received NHS treatment in the form of hormone therapy and supportive psychotherapy and had been living as a woman for eight years. It added:

> When the applicant embarked upon the treatment she was informed and/or was led to believe that this was a course of treatment that, dependant on medical recommendation, would be completed with reassignment surgery.

As a consequence:

> The health authority refusal leaves her still suffering from gender identity dysphoria, effectively in the middle of treatment and in an acutely distressing mental and physical state. It affects the applicant in every facet of her life but in particular the applicant is prevented and/or disadvantaged in her return to the labour market because of her continuing condition.

The patient's counsel wished to argue that having started a course of treatment she had a legitimate expectation that it should be completed:

> … having embarked on what she was informed and/or was given reason to believe, was a course of treatment culminating in surgery, whose consequences now are irreversible, [the patient] has a legitimate expectation and/or fairness requires that the treatment is completed in the absence of any countervailing public interest …

The health authority's counsel, however, did not consider the patient's application likely to succeed on grounds of 'legitimate expectation', because:

- there was no evidence that the health authority or anybody acting on its behalf had ever led the patient to believe that if she successfully undertook the various preliminaries medically required, the operation would be funded

- a challenge based on 'legitimate expectation' may succeed where a person has committed himself to a certain course of action on the basis of a policy or practice that is then changed before the course of action is complete.

The health authority's counsel concluded:

> *Accordingly, even though [patient's name] undoubtedly had a hope, and maybe also an expectation, I do not consider that any such expectation was 'legitimate' as against the authority, in the sense in which this term of art is used in public law.*

A further point to note in connection with the length of time the patient had been in contact with the health authority is that this may have been used in the judicial review to support an argument for funding surgery. In the opinion of the health authority's counsel:

> *If, however, the Applicant does succeed (as on my present incomplete information appears to me reasonably likely), the court would probably give a strong indication that among the other factors the authority should consider seriously is the fact that the Applicant has now waited almost five years (longer by the time of any hearing), for an operation for which she has been preparing for nine years.*

The length of 'waiting time' for a patient was important because although this is usually considered by health authorities to be an implicit rather than explicit way of rationing or prioritising treatment, it appeared to be considered an appropriate explicit way in the eyes of the court. In other words, the legal understanding of how a priority should be managed may be different to that of a health authority. This is made clear in the advice given by the health authority's counsel:

> No court would contest the authority's right to set the priority for gender reassignment surgery lower than, e.g. life-threatening conditions, or conditions which unless treated with reasonable speed will have irreversibly disabling effects. But the authority appears to adopt a different approach to the issue of 'priority' from the one which I consider would be adopted by the courts. The courts would be unlikely to interfere with a rationally based policy which gave an individual request for sex reassignment a lower priority, in terms of waiting time, than other treatments. But the authority's approach seems to be concerned with the general priority of sex reassignment as opposed to other forms of treatment ...

In this case expert advice was clearly of great importance. This was of two kinds, legal and clinical. The value of the legal advice was that it led the health authority to seek further clinical advice. The legal advisers asked for further information in several areas including the policies of other health authorities and it was during this investigation that the Charing Cross protocol was located.

In fact the legal advice was useful to the health authority in a way which was unexpected. It not only highlighted flaws in its policy but also contributed to its knowledge of the subject. The advice enabled the health authority to gain a deeper understanding of the ethical issues involved by bringing a different perspective to the issue of priority setting. It also prompted a wider search for evidence of the cost effectiveness of gender reassignment surgery, and for intelligence about the policies of other health authorities.

As a result of the legal challenge, the health authority clarified its ECR protocol and procedure for dealing with appeals against refusals to fund treatment. Although a protocol drafted five years earlier had included an appeals procedure for patients when funding had been refused, this was not being used and 'needed confirmation and implementation'. The reworded document which was given approval at a health authority meeting included statements that individual requests would be assessed on their own merits and that it was clinical need and urgency which determined whether approval was given and not financial considerations. It also described the process for patients wishing to lodge an appeal.

This case received very little publicity and the approach adopted by the press was factual rather than emotive. The Chief Executive considered that the public would be in favour of a low priority being given to gender reassignment surgery and so there would not have been public criticism of the health authority's refusal to fund the treatment. This raises ethical issues related to fairness and equity of treatment. There may be a tendency for a health authority to ensure it has careful procedures for conditions that evoke public sympathy. Certainly until this case, the health authority had an explicit procedure for considering the individual circumstances of those requesting ECRs for IVF, but not gender reassignment surgery. The implication is that treatments deemed to have low priority should always be accompanied by a procedure for taking into account the circumstances of individuals if equity objectives are to be achieved.

Summary

- Legal advice may identify weaknesses in health authority decision-making.

- It is important that a health authority demonstrates that a blanket ban is not in operation.

- There is value in carrying out research to find out what other health authorities are doing.

- Expert advice can be critical in providing policies or protocols that carry eligibility criteria, and enabling an assessment of procedures in terms of cost effectiveness.

Case 4

Key points

- Patient with multiple sclerosis.

- Patient was prescribed beta-interferon by consultant neurologist.

- Trust pharmacy refused to supply the prescription as it was outside the budget allocation.

- The HA refused to make additional money available for beta-interferon unless part of randomised controlled trial.

- Patient's father publicised case and took it to judicial review.

- The court found against the HA.

- HA instructed to release funds for beta-interferon.

Outline of events

This case involved a patient who was diagnosed as having the relapsing/remitting form of multiple sclerosis in 1987. In January 1996 the patient was referred to a consultant neurologist who assessed him as suitable for a new drug called beta-interferon, which was reported to slow down the degenerative progress of the disease. The patient took his prescription to the trust's pharmacy but the drug was 'red lined' to prevent prescription without permission because it was costly and may not have been covered in the existing block contract for neurology. This meant that the patient could not obtain the drug.

The patient's father wrote to the Chief Executive of the trust who explained that the drug was new and not covered within the existing contract they had with the health authority. The patient's father then contacted the health authority believed to be responsible, the local press and his MPs. As the patient did not actually live within the catchment area of this particular health authority, there was a delay before the appropriate authority was notified.

This early confusion meant that the patient and his family were 'passed around' before coming into contact with the responsible health authority. It also meant the health authority concerned was propelled into the middle of a situation that had already been developing for some time. As the Chief Executive said:

> There were all sorts of confusions about who should do what and I think the internal market has a lot to answer for. The very mechanisms created around it are confusing to the patient ... As soon as it was realised he lived in [area] he was directed to us and I had a number of discussions with the Chief Executive of the [trust] to catch up on the situation. A lot of this was water under the bridge by the time I got hold of it and the expectations were there and if you like the problem had already matured by the time we got involved.

The health authority had already carried out discussions with local professional groups about beta-interferon as a general issue. This was in response to an executive letter from the Department of Health (EL[95]97) and, following extensive publicity about the new drug, warnings from the NHS Executive Regional Office that it would be an important issue. The local professional groups consulted had been against giving priority to the introduction of beta-interferon.

In addition, the health authority had received advice from the region's directors of public health and from the School for Health and Related Research (SCHARR) at Sheffield University. This advice seemed to point in the same direction. As the Chief Executive explained:

... basically the advice that was being received from both the public health people and from SCHARR was that this was an unproven new drug and that how it was introduced should be treated with great care. If at all possible it should be part of a research study because otherwise we would never find out if it was any use at all.

The Director of Public Health provided a more detailed explanation:

There was quite a lot of debate in the professional groups about whether the drug was effective. There seemed to be quite a lot of criticism of the trials in various articles, certainly about them being stopped short, and about whether something which was statistically significant was clinically significant ... There was a clear feeling among the Directors of Public Health and other professionals that it was most appropriate to use it in clinical trials.

As a result the health authority board made a decision not to give beta-interferon high priority. It agreed to put £50,000 into the ECR budget specifically identified for the drug, with the aim of ensuring that any patients introduced to beta-interferon were in trials. The Chief Executive summed up the health authority's position:

The upshot was that all the professional advisory groups were very much against giving priority to beta-interferon being introduced. At the time it's relevant to say there was extreme financial pressure – it's less now than it was – at the time we were struggling and had a big deficit to cope with. It wasn't just theoretical. So the important thing is that the GPs in particular were adamantly, in the context that I describe, against us giving any priority to this drug; so much so that they'd have given us a really hard time if we did.

When the health authority became aware that the issue was no longer a general or hypothetical one but a specific case which needed a decision, it re-examined the advice it had received and went back to the advisory groups. As the Chief Executive put it, group participants:

thrashed it round and round to work out what was the right thing to do in the circumstances.

The issue was taken to a health authority board meeting and the decision made was that the policy should remain unchanged. The Chief Executive wrote to the patient explaining the decision not to give the drug priority and stating that it would not be funded unless it was part of a research trial. The patient's father wanted to pursue the matter further and so was invited to a meeting. Much of the discussion at the meeting was around the scientific evidence for the drug's effectiveness. According to the Chief Executive:

> *... a lot of what we discussed was not around preventing the son having the appropriate treatment but around the very confused scientific evidence as we understood it, about whether the drug was beneficial or not and the very serious side effects which were a risk within it.*

Although there was a majority view in the health authority, there was some disagreement among those involved in the discussions. The Chief Executive's position was that the individual patient had been led to believe he was going to receive the drug. This meant the health authority had a moral obligation to supply it. The majority view was that the general principle was more important. As the Chief Executive explained:

> *... I think the biggest concern I had was that the individual patient had been led to believe that he was going to get the drug and I felt we had some moral obligation for that reason which was different from the matter of principle but in discussing it more widely with other people it was felt this was outweighed by the broader issue. I personally found it very difficult to accept. I mean this poor person was clutching at straws, they're offered the straw and then it appears to be dashed away from them.*

The patient received a letter from the trust notifying him of the decision not to fund the treatment in November 1996, and as a result the family applied for a judicial review. This went to the court in July 1997.

The issues were identified as follows:

- whether the DoH Circular EL(95)97 constituted *directions* which the health authority concerned was under a duty to apply, or merely *guidance*

- whether the health authority had acted unlawfully in adopting a policy not to fund the treatment of relapsing/remitting multiple sclerosis with beta-interferon

- whether the applicant had a legitimate expectation of treatment with beta-interferon based on a decision communicated to him by a letter dated 19 February 1996, that whether he received treatment would be a clinical decision, that decision having already been made in his favour.

The main argument of the counsel for the plaintiff was that the health authority did not follow the Department of Health guidance. In sticking to the line that it would only fund beta-interferon as part of a trial, the health authority was not carrying out the request that it should:

> develop and implement local arrangements to manage the entry of such drugs into the NHS in consultation with other key interests, especially GPs and patient interest groups; and in particular, to initiate and continue prescribing of beta-interferon through hospitals.

This was because there was no clinical trial in operation and so the health authority position constituted in effect a blanket ban.

The counsel for the plaintiff also made much of the fact that the health authority Chief Executive, in a letter replying to an MP who was acting on the patient's behalf in February 1996, had said that the health authority was following guidance by 'discussing the contractual arrangements with local neurology provider units' and so:

> *priority for use of the limited funds available will be determined by the neurologists at the specialist centres and whether [the patient] receives this treatment will be a clinical decision.*

In fact, argued the patient's counsel, the health authority did not have any discussions with the trust about contractual arrangements.

There was also evidence that health authorities in the region concerned were in the process of revising an earlier position on beta-interferon. This was mentioned in a letter the patient received after writing to the then Prime Minister, John Major. His letter of reply in September 1996, stated:

> *... I understand that the [region's] health authorities have recently reviewed their position and are making arrangements for the treatment to be prescribed in appropriate cases. The proposed national trial has been postponed indefinitely ... I hope that this is helpful in explaining the situation and that given the revised position of health authorities in [the region], it may now be possible for [patient] to be treated with beta-interferon.*

In addition, on 10 October 1996, the Medical Director of the NHS Executive notified all health authorities that the proposed trials had been postponed indefinitely, adding:

> *there was now no further reason for delaying the introduction of local purchasing policies in line with the Circular.*

However, following a meeting between the health authority's Chief Executive and Director of Public Health, the trust Chief Executive and the patient's father, a letter was written to the patient by the trust Chief Executive on 18 November 1996 stating:

> … the policy of [the health authority] was that they could not support, in cost effective terms, the use of the drug beta-interferon for relapsing multiple sclerosis patients and also they could not identify any new money to give priority to the use of this drug.

The counsel for the plaintiff argued that new money could be identified and this was the £50,000 which had been set aside by the health authority for the ECR budget to fund beta-interferon.

The health authority's counsel argued that:

- the Executive Letter was meant as guidance only and it was up to health authorities to make local decisions about how guidance should be implemented

- the health authority did not have a blanket ban because there was a patient receiving beta-interferon in its catchment area

- the health authority would not spend the £50,000 without inclusion within a clinical trial because there was no other way of distributing the money fairly. A 'first come first served' basis was not equitable. All existing eligible patients would have to be clinically assessed and it was not clear how this could be carried out in a way which remained within the allocated budget

- health authorities were under a statutory duty not to overspend

- clinical decisions must always be taken with due regard to resources available.

The court found that the health authority's policy in 1996 for funding beta-interferon for multiple sclerosis was unlawful. In his summing up, the judge said:

> I conclude therefore that the policy was unlawful because it was not a proper application of the guidance contained in the Circular, and the respondents did not properly take into account the essential requirements of the Circular in adopting and maintaining their policy. In my judgment, the respondents were aware from an early stage that they were not applying or taking account of the Circular. They knew that their own policy amounted to a blanket ban on beta-interferon treatment. A blanket ban was the very antithesis of national policy, whose aim was to target the drug appropriately at patients who were most likely to benefit from treatment.

The health authority was required within 14 days to formulate and implement a policy for the funding of beta-interferon for multiple sclerosis that complied with the NHS Executive's Circular.

The decision was a shock to the health authority, which thought it would win the case. As the Chief Executive put it:

> We got legal advice … they said all the way until the last day that we had a very good case … My understanding of judicial reviews is that they are based around the decision-making process rather than the decision. Have you done it fairly and so on … looking back on ours, we'd given it hours and hours of all the right people's time and I was fairly confident that although they might not have liked the decision, it was properly considered by the proper people with the legal authority to do so.

As a result of the court decision, the health authority reconsidered its position and the patient received the treatment.

Analysis of events

As in the Taxol case (Case 2) the patient and relatives in this case were led by the hospital specialists to believe the drug would be prescribed. From the patient's point of view, the drug had been recommended as one that would help him manage his condition. His consultant wanted him to have it but the 'authorities' would not fund it because sufficient funds were not available.

The meeting between the patient's father, the health authority's Chief Executive, Director of Public Health and trust Chief Executive did not resolve this issue. Although those involved in the meeting explained that their decision was based on the fact that the available evidence suggested the new drug was not clinically effective, this was in conflict with the opinion of the patient's consultant. Given the circumstances, it was understandable that the patient would wish to try and obtain a drug that offered even a small hope of improving his deteriorating condition.

The key to this case lies in the fact that the health authority and consultants in the trust had no agreement on the introduction of beta-interferon. In this there are again similarities with the Taxol case (Case 2). Here the health authority had consulted widely with appropriate clinical groups but individual clinicians had not recognised the legitimacy of the decision made as a result of this consultation nor had they been involved in working out how the drug would be managed at the level of individual patients. The health authority had accepted a policy that beta-interferon would only be prescribed as part of a clinical trial, but individual consultants were prescribing it outside a trial.

The conflict was further compounded by apparent differences between advice issued by expert groups and that provided by the NHS Executive. The advice offered by the School for Health and Related Research (SCHARR) at Sheffield University, was that this was a drug which should be introduced only as part of a clinical trial, but the Circular (EL[95]97) released by the NHS Executive advised health authorities to develop and implement a local prescribing approach to the drug which targeted the drug appropriately at patients who were most likely to benefit from the treatment. The health authority argued that the best way to accomplish this was to prescribe the drug only as part of a trial and this meant waiting for the proposed national trial to begin before releasing £50,000 which had been put aside to purchase beta-interferon. However, the patient's counsel argued successfully that this position did not adequately fulfil the NHS Executive's requirements as set out in the Circular. As the High Court judge stated:

> I do not consider that the respondents' policy could at any time have fairly been described as a reasonable way of giving effect to the Circular. The respondents, like others, no doubt honestly and conscientiously believed that the efficacy of beta-interferon had not been sufficiently tested. The assumption that underpinned the Circular was that it had been sufficiently tested...This is not a case in which a health authority departed from the national policy because there were special factors which it considered exceptionally justified departure. The respondents failed to implement any aspect of national policy, principally because they disagreed with it altogether.

The judge added that once it had been announced in October 1996 that the proposed national trial was to be postponed indefinitely, the health authority's policy became unlawful. This was because:

> Once there was no trial in prospect, in truth the respondents had no policy at all in relation to the implementation of the Circular, and yet they continued to maintain this unsustainable position.

The health authority did not change its position because it could not find a way to prescribe the drug in a fair and equitable manner. Allowing patients to be prescribed the drug on a 'first come, first served' basis was not considered to be acceptable because it would not achieve the aim of prescribing the drug according to clinical need. The health authority was unable to work with clinicians to find a more acceptable set of criteria. This meant that the counsel for the patient was able to argue successfully that the health authority had a blanket ban on the prescription of beta-interferon. The fact that there was one patient within the health authority's area who was receiving beta-interferon was not considered to be a legitimate rebuttal of this position because, as there was no policy which would have allowed him through the net, the inference was that he slipped through unnoticed by the health authority.

The legal advice provided to the health authority in this case did not suggest that it needed to re-examine or strengthen its decision-making on the issue. Instead the health authority's legal advisors suggested it was in a strong position. The health authority's understanding that a judicial review would base its judgement on the process rather than the decision was correct. But process and decision were not easily separated in this instance. The High Court took the unusual step of finding in favour of the patient because the health authority decided not to follow the Circular which in the words of the judge 'is something they were not entitled to do'.

The health authority felt that the Department of Health and NHS Executive Regional Office had sent 'mixed messages' in advice it received. As the Chief Executive explained:

> The Department of Health's Medical Adviser sent very mixed messages. He both offered support and said we should have implemented the Circular. The Regional Office also sent mixed messages. They never said we should back off and they supported us going to the judicial review.

The health authority did not consider that it had a weak case or had been in the wrong but believed it had lost the case as a result of being sent contradictory advice by the Department of Health.

Summary

- As in other cases reported here, a health authority can find itself in the middle of a dispute without warning.

- A patient can end up being 'passed around' so it is difficult for him or her to find out who is responsible for making a decision.

- Conflicting messages sent out by drug companies, consultants, trusts and health authorities can confuse the patient and result in the breakdown of relations between NHS and patient.

- If health authorities and trusts do not work together they open themselves up to inconsistencies in the way treatment is provided.

- If a health authority appears to have a 'blanket ban' it is likely to lose a judicial review.

- Good legal advice (scrutinising and critical, not overly supportive) is important in securing a successful outcome if a judicial review is pending.

Case 5

Key points

- Child with haemophilia A who started on factor VIII but developed inhibitors.

- HA asked to fund a high dose factor VIII tolerance induction regimen.

- HA established expert panel, which included clinical and economic advisers.

- Experts came up with alternative way of reducing intolerance, which was as effective but cost less.

- HA agreed to fund the alternative treatment.

- HA and trust agreed to share the cost on a 50/50 basis.

- Patient and family had no knowledge of the discussion and no contact with the HA.

Outline of events

This case involved an eight-year-old child with haemophilia A who started on factor VIII but developed inhibitors or antibodies for factor VIII so that it lost its effect. The child was having haemorrhages in the joints, which are extremely painful in the short term and severely reduce the quality of life. In the long term they can lead to disability.

The health authority first heard about the case when it was contacted in June 1994 by the patient's consultant at a local trust. As the Director of Public Health explained:

What they were proposing was a flooding type of treatment where they give very high dose factor VIII, which is expensive anyway, and overwhelm the body's ability to produce antibodies so that the patient develops a tolerance to the drug. It is a fairly well-established immunologic technique in a general sense, but there is a limited amount of evidence of its effectiveness in the case of factor VIII. The cost of the course would be half a million pounds for one year.

The health authority set up an expert panel with the aim of assessing the potential benefit of the treatment to the individual set against the opportunity cost of funding it compared with other interventions. The panel was a joint trust and health authority one and included a representative from the Royal College of Pathologists (a haematologist). It also requested advice from the Health Economics Research Group at Brunel University. The haematologist reviewed the literature and then the expert panel contacted an immunologist. He suggested another way of reducing tolerance, through a slightly higher dose of factor VIII coupled with a drug to suppress the immune system. This cost approximately £100,000 for a year's treatment.

The information collected was given to the health economists and they produced a table for the analysis of the two options in terms of cost as well as effectiveness. The Director of Public Health considered that the health economists' report:

... enabled us to compare the two treatments in a health economics sense and gave a feel for how this compared with other dimensions. There was a consensus that we should recommend using the less expensive treatment which appeared to be probably equally efficacious but considerably cheaper...fortunately it did not appear to be a matter of saying this is less effective but cheaper, which would have made it a more difficult decision. So I think the panel was able to feel reasonably happy making that recommendation.

The recommendations of the expert panel went to a health authority board meeting and were ratified. This followed the practice in which cases where the costs were high, or which were difficult or unclear because of the ethical issues involved, were taken to the health authority in an anonymous form for discussion and approval. The patient received the treatment and he and his family were not aware that the health authority had discussed the issues. This was because the health authority had no contact with the family involved. As the Director of Public Health explained:

> *The health authority's perspective is that it's not our role to involve the family. We try not to get involved in discussions about individual patients or families. That's a clinical issue.*

There was some discussion about whether the Haemophilia Society should be involved but the health authority decided that it preferred not to involve them in discussions about individual patients and would rather involve them in developing guidelines.

The health authority had also been involved in developing an explicit priority-setting framework, using a set of values that was similar to those suggested by the NHS Executive. It had weighted these and placed a higher value on cost effectiveness than the other principles. It had also drawn up a framework to enable it to use the values in a scoring system. As the Director of Public Health explained:

> *… what we are trying to do is work on the application of the explicit priority-setting framework – how you weight the variables and what is the process by which we identify the disinvestments.*

The case raised two important issues for the health authority. The first was the issue of risk sharing on high cost treatments. In this case it was agreed that the health authority and trust should share the cost of the treatment. The Director of Public Health put it this way:

Should purchasers and providers share the risks of these high cost cases? In this case we simply split it 50/50 but there are various ways it can be done – joining a consortium, paying into an insurance fund, etc.

The second issue was about new treatments and what counts as adequate evidence. In this case the evidence for the effectiveness of the proposed treatment was not very strong and there was disagreement about the relative benefits, but there was another treatment that seemed to be as effective and was cheaper. The health authority had a choice of treatment and was able to reach a satisfactory decision because of this. The health authority had a new drugs panel, which decided what counted as effective evidence. The Director of Public Health described how this worked and how they wanted to develop the process:

They work using implicit criteria which are shared by other members of the committee. It ought to be possible to develop some principles that could obviously not be applied in a mechanistic way but could be used as guides. It's a matter of trying to map, if you like, the decision-making processes that are used by experienced senior clinicians who are involved. We could have a set of principles that the health authority agrees with and the clinicians agree with. There would still be a huge amount of judgement involved and what this will need to take into account is the values, needless to say, because the strength of the evidence is one issue but also equity is involved. If you happen to get a rare disease, the chances of there being adequate evidence are less, simply because it is a rare disease. So should you be penalised in terms of capacity to benefit? You would have to have a sliding scale, so the rarer the disease, the lower the standards of evidence required. That is one equity issue. Another is … the existence of other treatments. Where there is no other treatment available, the standard of evidence should be less.

The patient received the treatment, which was successful in overcoming his tolerance to factor VIII and enabled him to continue to manage the haemophilia.

Analysis of events

This case is different from the other examples included in that the relationship between the patient and the NHS did not break down. The patient and his family knew nothing about the health authority's discussion of the issues. Were the decision to have taken more time, or had the health authority refused to fund the treatment, there may have been more points of similarity with the other cases discussed here. As it stands, it would appear that from the patient's point of view the process ran smoothly and the outcome was acceptable.

Expert panel

Two key aspects contributed to this outcome. The first, identified by the health authority's Director of Public Health, was the expert panel set up to investigate the merits and demerits of funding treatment for the particular patient in question. This comprised managers from the trust involved, the health authority, the patient's clinician who wanted to prescribe factor VIII, and a haematologist from the Royal College of Pathologists. An immunologist and a group of health economists were also called on to provide advice. This panel of people brought together independent experts who could examine the treatment from a number of different perspectives (clinical appropriateness and cost effectiveness) and those who were involved at the local level. Together they were able to reach a mutually acceptable decision about treatment.

The Director of Public Health was convinced the panel was crucial in helping them to reach a decision. He said:

> I think the benefit of having a panel, which I think is also something that came out of the Child B case, in terms of seeking external

advice, was one of the lessons we learned. In our case I don't think the clinician concerned knew about the other therapy. It was through the application of a number of minds to the problem that the other options were arrived at.

Co-operation

The second key aspect was the way the health authority and trust worked together, starting with the panel, and continuing through the sharing of the financial costs involved in providing the treatment.

The health authority had learned from the case and similar ones in that it was attempting to apply an explicit priority-setting framework to funding issues. Instead of leaving the values at a general level, it had worked on translating the terms into criteria against which services and treatments could be assessed. For example, the health authority had decided that effective resource use was more important than the other values and this was divided into three elements:

- potential health gain or efficacy

- economy or efficiency

- strength of evidence.

The other values were access, equity and responsiveness. Each could be used as a measure by using a scale of 1–5, for example, scoring whether for a particular treatment/service access was worsened or improved, or whether it provided temporary relief or was life saving (efficacy), and so on.

The health authority also had a policy of not totally excluding particular services from funding. Instead, it was encouraging the development of guidelines in the form of clinical scoring systems, as a means of setting priorities within major programmes and supporting clinical decisions about the appropriateness of treatment. Very high cost cases not covered by the agreed programme guidelines were referred to the health authority for discussion, as in the factor VIII case described. As part of the process of establishing guidelines to try and manage the possible future unexpected high cost of new treatments, the health authority was also planning to work with clinicians to develop principles for assessing the effectiveness of new drugs and treatments.

Summary

- Decisions which do not involve the patient and family are relatively simple compared with those that do, in part because of the consequent lack of publicity about the case.

- An expert panel can play a crucial role in that they can investigate the issues from different perspectives and present a coherent argument to the health authority concerned.

- When a trust and health authority work together to find a solution it can bring benefits to both, such as sharing the cost of treatment.

- Some health authorities are working on the application of a priority-setting framework and exploring ways of establishing principles for assessing the effectiveness of new drugs and treatments.

Chapter 3

Analysis

The five cases described here illustrate that the dilemmas raised by the Child B case (Ham and Pickard, 1998) are not unique. Although each of these cases is different from that of Child B, and indeed from one other, there are a number of common themes (see Table 1). In this chapter we move on from the descriptions offered in Chapter 2 to discuss these issues and to identify points of comparison with the Child B case. The analysis covers:

- the role of patients and their families

- the response of health authorities

- the role of clinicians

- the involvement of the courts

- the role of the Department of Health

- the role of the media

- the ethical dilemmas of priority setting.

Table 1 Case study analysis

Case	Patient/family	Health authority	Clinicians	Courts	Department of Health
Case 1	Family disagree with clinical diagnosis. MP supports family. They go elsewhere for treatment. What are the child's best interests?	HA did not meet family. Lots of local publicity. Values framework enabled decision to be made. Funding not provided on grounds that inappropriate and not in interests of child.	Disagreement between US and UK cancer specialists.	Not involved.	Involved. Gave advice on need for clear process and values framework. Emphasised local responsibility.
Case 2	Patient believes treatment is her only option but funding is not available. Contacts media to get funding and treatment she needs.	HA did not meet patient. Lots of local publicity. Confusion over funding. Funding provided after expert advice enables individual exception to be made.	No clinical disagreement. Dispute over evidence for benefit of Taxol for this condition. Key role of independent expert.	Not involved.	Regional Office involved. Gave advice on need for independent expert. Drew out lessons for other HAs.
Case 3	Patient believes only surgery will help her. Despite persistence, she cannot get HA to fund it so she resorts to legal advice. MP supports patient.	HA did not meet patient – lots of letters. HA receives solicitor's letter, reviews own case and finds it weak so seeks advice. Agrees to fund on policy enabling individual exceptions to be made.	Evidence of effectiveness unclear or not widely understood. Clinicians may disagree, but more a disagreement over limits of NHS funding. Importance of Charing Cross protocol.	Judicial review threatened.	Not involved.
Case 4	Family felt that they had been promised treatment for their son. Family were 'passed around' between organisations. Contact media, MP, to help them get funding for treatment. They win court case and get treatment.	HA meets father. Lots of local publicity. Confusion over funding. HA implements national guidance in own way and refused to fund. Courts force change of decision.	Disagreement/ confusion amongst local specialists. Disagreement between GPs and specialists. Some dispute over evidence.	Judicial review over-turned HA's decision.	Involved. Sent 'mixed messages' to HA.
Case 5	Family not aware of discussions/not involved.	No publicity. HA and trust work together. Agree to fund alternative treatment. HA and trust share costs.	Disagreement over evidence. Expert panel identifies alternatives. Clinicians and economists work together.	Not involved.	Not involved.
Case 6 **Child B**	Father disagrees with clinical diagnosis. They go elsewhere for treatment. What are the child's best interests?	HA did not meet patient. Lots of publicity. Judicial review forces examination of decision-making process. Confusion over role of finances. HA does not fund.	Clinical disagreement between adult and child cancer specialists and private and NHS sectors.	Judicial review endorsed HA's decision.	Involved. Emphasised local responsibility.

The role of patients and families

All these examples, with the exception of Case 5, testify to the decline in deference on the part of patients and families and their willingness to challenge decisions with which they disagree. In Case 1, disagreement between the family of the child with a malignant brain tumour and the UK specialist responsible for the child's treatment resulted in the family travelling to the USA with the cost of care being met by public support from the local community. This case offers the closest parallel with that of Child B in that the health authority supported the view of the clinicians who knew the patient and the family and declined to provide funding for a treatment that was seen as experimental and having a low probability of success. Other parallels with the Child B case were that trust between the UK specialist and the family broke down, thereby reinforcing the family's quest for further advice and clinical opinions, and there were disagreements over what course of action was in the best interests of the patient. In both of these cases, the dissatisfaction of the parents of the children involved led to the search for treatments outside the UK, illustrating the lengths to which families are prepared to go in these circumstances.

Cases 2, 3 and 4 are different in that patients and families were challenging the refusal of health authorities to fund treatment recommended by clinicians rather than questioning the decisions of clinicians themselves. In all three cases, the challenges were successful, although the health authorities concerned changed their decisions for different reasons and with varying degrees of reluctance. The alliance between patients and clinicians appears to have been of significance in these cases in producing the outcome sought by patients and their families, although in itself this was not sufficient. What was also important was the involvement of other actors in support of the challenge to health authority decisions.

This was expressed in the use of the media to publicise the circumstances of patients in some cases and also the involvement of

MPs. Even more important was the willingness of patients and families to either invoke legal action or to contemplate it against a background, as we note below, of the UK courts being reluctant traditionally to overturn either health authority or medical decisions. In their different ways, these actions underline the increasing assertiveness of patients and those acting as their advocates and the need therefore for health authorities and others charged with making decisions on the funding of treatment to ensure that these decisions are well founded and defensible.

The response of health authorities

As the organisations responsible for policy-making and priority setting at a local level, the health authorities found themselves having to review and defend their decisions and to account for the actions they had taken. Our research has revealed that responsibility within health authorities was shared between the board, as the body ultimately charged with determining policies and priorities, and senior managers, among whom the chief executive and especially the director of public health were the most significant.

Decisions on individual cases such as those reviewed here are usually delegated from the board to senior managers and it is often the director of public health and his or her colleagues who are responsible for these decisions. In circumstances when it is anticipated that cases may give rise to media and public interest or may raise wider issues of policy then it is not unusual for these staff to bring them to the attention of chief executives and other board members.

This is what happened in the Child B case and in that case it was the director of public health, the chief executive and the authority's chairman, in discussion with the head of administration, who decided what should be done. The five cases reviewed here were handled in a similar way. Directors of public health, as the chief medical advisers to health authorities, were more often than not in the lead, and took a view on the cases concerned in the light of their review of the literature and evidence and the framework for priority setting agreed by the boards of their authorities.

Sometimes these frameworks set out explicit principles intended to inform decision-making, as in the example of Case 1 where the values framework adopted by the health authority was used to weigh up the different considerations involved in the decision not to fund further aggressive treatment of a malignant brain tumour. In other cases, the frameworks were more general, and the experience of resolving these cases often stimulated health authorities to be more explicit and specific about the basis on which they set priorities. As in the Child B case, the use of a values framework, entailing the application of criteria such as appropriateness, effectiveness and responsiveness to decisions of this kind, was found to be helpful in testing out alternatives and arriving at robust and consistent choices.

While public health directors were central to these cases, they were not the only individuals involved within health authorities. Chief executives were often drawn in when the wider significance of the cases became apparent, often illustrated by the interest of the media, MPs and the Department of Health. In some cases the boards of the health authorities also played a part. These cases therefore differed from that of Child B where only the authority chairman among the non-executive members was involved.

Apart from illustrating local variation in decision-making processes, this suggests that the increasing attention given to the refusal to fund treatment is leading to decisions being tested at the highest level within health authorities. Part of the purpose of this is to generate board level ownership and support for these decisions. As such, our study indicates that health authorities are responding to the concerns expressed by some analysts of the Child B case to the effect that the lack of involvement of the board was a weakness in that case (Wall, 1995).

Direct communication

Direct communication between health authority staff and patients and their families was not in itself sufficient to overcome the disagreement that arose over treatment decisions. This was illustrated in Case 4 where a meeting between the health authority and the family did not prevent the case going to court. The health authorities involved in the other cases made the point that with hindsight they might have communicated more effectively with those affected by their decisions. But there may be limits to which face-to-face discussions and the opportunity to receive a direct explanation of the basis of decisions will succeed in compensating for outcomes other than those sought unless there is scope for these decisions to be changed. This is an important conclusion in view of the finding of the Child B study that the Cambridge and Huntingdon Health Authority was vulnerable to criticism for its failure to allow the Bowen family direct access to decision-makers.

Limited opportunity for appeal

The opportunity for patients and families to appeal against health authority decisions was limited. Only in Case 3 did an appeals procedure exist, but even here the procedure had fallen into disuse and the challenge of the patient to the decision not to fund surgery for gender reassignment forced the health authority to review this procedure and reinforce its importance. As in the Child B case, this indicates that health authorities may need to consider strengthening their decision-making arrangements by building in opportunity for appeals. This is reinforced by the focus of the courts on the way in which decisions are reached and the need for health authorities to show that they have considered relevant facts and treated each case on its merits.

It is clear that the health authorities used a range of informal and *ad hoc* review procedures, and in three cases the outcome was to change the original decision in favour of patients and families. In these cases, a review of the evidence on effectiveness was instrumental in leading to the change of approach. To this extent, the challenge of patients, supported by specialists and independent advisers, threw up new evidence and led the health authorities to reconsider their policies.

The role of clinicians

Clinicians were closely involved in the resolution of these cases both in recommending treatment options for patients and in serving as independent advisers when disputes arose. We have noted already that an important difference between these cases and that of Child B was that clinicians tended to support patients in their quest for treatment and this meant that they became embroiled in debate with the health authorities. Having made this point, it should also be noted that a similarity with the Child B case is that the health authorities then sought independent clinical advice in seeking to resolve this debate.

In Case 1, this advice confirmed the view that further intensive treatment was not appropriate, while in the other four cases the involvement of outside advisers lent support to the original clinical opinion. The main exception was Case 4, where the health authority maintained its opposition to the funding of beta-interferon for a patient with multiple sclerosis as the weight of advice it received from local professionals and independent experts was that this treatment was unproven in its effectiveness and should only be offered in the context of a clinical trial. In the three other cases, independent advice was instrumental in prompting the health authorities to reconsider their decisions.

In Case 2, a clinician consulted by the health authority at the suggestion of the Regional Director of Public Health supported the view that Taxol should be used for the treatment of ovarian cancer and this advice was accepted. In Case 3, the health authority sought information from other health authorities about the funding of gender reassignment surgery and in the process came across the

Charing Cross protocol. This enabled it to change its original decision not to fund surgery but to do so within a framework that ensured that resources were used on patients who would benefit. The resolution of Case 5 was also affected by independent advice with an immunologist and haematologist both offering alternatives to the treatment option that had been proposed for a patient with haemophilia. In this instance, as in Case 3, health economists were also asked for their opinions.

A distinctive feature of Case 5 was the joint approach adopted by the health authority and the NHS trust involved. This, together with the contribution made by independent advisers, enabled the issue to be handled in a collaborative manner and without the conflict that arose in the other cases. In Case 5, the consensus between independent experts helped the health authority to resolve the issue, while the absence of consensus in other cases accentuated the difficulties that arose. This was particularly apparent in Case 1, where there was disagreement between UK and US specialists, and Case 4, where the evidence on beta-interferon was interpreted differently by clinicians. The contrast between Case 4 and Case 5 is important in showing that when local clinicians and health authorities fail to work together patients tend to be caught in the crossfire, whereas when there is collaboration this can be avoided.

It is difficult to set priorities and make decisions in individual cases simply on the basis of evidence. There is a cautionary tale here for the advocates of evidence-based medicine. This is reinforced by the Child B case where the clinicians involved not only disagreed about the evidence on treatment outcomes but also drew quite different conclusions from it about the implications for intervention. As our study and the Child B case demonstrate, these issues are particularly challenging in the case of experimental treatments. In view of the skill needed in interpreting the available evidence, Case 2 illustrates the role an independent clinician can play in explaining to patients directly the complexities of treatment decisions.

The involvement of the courts

The decline of deference on the part of patients and families is linked to the increasing involvement of the courts in challenges to decisions not to fund treatment. This was most apparent in Case 4 where the High Court ruled in favour of the patient and required the health authority to review its decision and find the resources to fund the use of beta-interferon for the treatment of multiple sclerosis. What was unusual about this case was the willingness of the courts to overturn a health authority decision in view of the well-established reluctance of judges in England to take this course.

The court's decision was prompted by the rigid policy adopted by the health authority and the conflict between this policy and the Circular issued by the Department of Health. This came as a surprise to the health authority, which felt that it had taken account of the Circular and arrived at a decision that was appropriate in the circumstances. Indeed, it had been encouraged by the Regional Office of the NHS Executive to defend its approach at a judicial review. The health authority came unstuck in this case because it did not apply the Circular appropriately and it was therefore vulnerable on procedural grounds.

The threat of legal action was also a consideration in Case 3. In this example, the health authority took legal advice when it received notification of a judicial review and found that its policy on the funding of gender reassignment was vulnerable to challenge in the courts. As in Case 4, one of the reasons for this was that the health authority appeared to have adopted a blanket ban in its policy on gender reassignment. In the light of this advice and the threat of being taken to court, the health authority reviewed both its policy and procedures and adopted an approach that meant that the case was resolved without the courts becoming involved. The possibility of legal action occurring was also a consideration in Case 2, where the health authority pre-empted this possibility by seeking independent advice.

These cases shed further light on the issues raised by the Child B case where ultimately the courts supported the health authority's decision not to fund treatment. Two points deserve emphasis:

- the importance of health authorities considering each case individually and not adopting policies on priority setting which are inflexible

- the significance of Case 4 in indicating that the courts may be more willing in future to question the basis of health authority decisions, especially when it can be shown that these decisions conflict with Department of Health guidance.

This is not to argue that the courts will seek to replace health authority judgements with their own, rather that those responsible for decision-making within the NHS will have to be even more careful in future to ensure that their policies and procedures do not fall foul of legal challenges.

One other point emerges from these examples that did not figure in the Child B case and that is the concept of 'legitimate expectation' on the part of patients. The lawyers involved in Cases 3 and 4 invoked this argument to suggest that a patient who was able to show that he or she had been promised a particular treatment had a right to expect that that treatment would be provided. Although not decisive in either case, this concept could be important in future if doctors determine that a certain course of action is clinically appropriate and that as a consequence a patient has built up expectations based on medical advice.

The role of the Department of Health

The Department of Health was involved in three of the five cases. This involvement was channelled through the Regional Office of the NHS Executive in Case 2 where the advice of the Regional Director of Public Health was seen to be constructive and helped the health authority resolve the conflict with the patient by seeking independent advice on the use of Taxol for the treatment of ovarian cancer. Subsequently, the lessons drawn from the handling of the case were disseminated throughout the region to assist other health authorities faced with similar choices.

The involvement of the Department of Health was perceived to be much less positive in Case 4. In particular, the health authority concerned felt that the Department was offering mixed messages on the use of beta-interferon for the treatment of multiple sclerosis and in difficult circumstances this made its job even harder. Indeed, the guidance eventually issued by the Department on beta-interferon was seen as decisive in the courts and was one of the key reasons why the health authority was asked to reconsider its decision to refuse to fund treatment.

The Department played a part in the background in Case 1. Its involvement here stemmed from the interest shown in the case by the local MP and the need for ministers and civil servants to be kept informed. The authority was given advice on how to handle the issue but as in the Child B case was left to determine what the outcome should be. In this process, the authority was advised of the lessons that had been learned from the Child B case and its use of a values framework in arriving at a decision was an example of this.

In none of these cases did the Department of Health directly overrule or question health authority decisions. Rather, consistent with the emphasis on local responsibility for decisions on priorities within a national policy framework, ministers and civil servants were content for the health authorities to determine the action to be taken. As in the Child B case, this can be interpreted as an appropriate use of delegated powers within a national system – or a convenient way of devolving blame for difficult and unpopular decisions. Certainly, the health authorities involved testified to the problems they had to confront in working through these cases, although if all issues of this kind were referred up the line for decision then it would rapidly overload the Department of Health.

The role of the media

A recurring theme in the reflections of health authority staff interviewed during this study was the intense media interest in some of these cases and the challenge of resolving them in the glare of publicity. In part, this can be explained in terms of the human interest associated with cases of this kind, involving both children and adults and often arising in life threatening circumstances when standard therapies had been exhausted. Child B may have been an extreme example of this but a number of the cases reported here also attracted considerable publicity. The health authorities confronted by media interest found that they had to spend a good deal of time answering questions and explaining the basis of their decisions and they were often thrust into this position with little notice and even less experience. By contrast, the health authority where media interest was non-existent, Case 5, was able to concentrate on responding to the patient and family and seeking the advice of clinicians, taking and reviewing decisions in a more measured and less pressurised environment.

Communicating the reasons for decisions to the media and the public was not easy when a number of considerations had to be balanced and when usually no single factor was decisive. Indeed, given that clinicians and independent advisors did not always agree, it was hardly surprising that the health authorities reported difficulties in putting their case across. Despite this, none of the authorities was subjected to the same degree of scrutiny and critical commentary experienced by the Cambridge and Huntingdon Health Authority in the Child B case. Part of the reason may have been that in all but Case 1 the authorities concerned eventually relented to the wishes of patients and families. And even in Case 1, the difficulty of determining the patient's best interests was recognised by the news reporters who followed the case and this had the effect of muting potential criticism.

The ethical dilemmas of priority setting

The issue of best interests highlights the underlying ethical dilemmas involved in priority setting. Where there is disagreement over the appropriate treatment of patients, and when children are not able to give consent, others have to make a judgement about what is in their best interests. In the Child B case, this issue became polarised around the views of Jaymee Bowen's father and the paediatricians who knew the family. The doctors felt unable to acquiesce to the father's wish to access further intensive treatment when in their judgement this was likely to result in more harm than benefit. Similar issues arose in Case 1 when the family of the child involved disputed the opinion of the UK specialists and, like Child B's father, were prepared to pursue their preferences until they obtained the treatment they were seeking.

More fundamentally, these cases illustrate the tension between a concern to do the best for individual patients and a desire to use scarce resources for the benefit of the population as a whole. This tension found expression in the differences that emerged between clinicians and health authorities. Perhaps not surprisingly, clinicians tended to act as agents and advocates of their patients, whereas health authorities took a wider perspective and arrived at decisions taking into account the opportunity costs involved in their choices, even though they rarely used this language. This meant that what appeared to be a rational use of resources from a population perspective ran counter to what appeared to be rational for individual patients. In these circumstances, particularly in the case of innovative treatments where there were doubts about effectiveness and when significant expenditure was involved, the health authorities were inclined to take a more critical view than clinicians of the balance between costs and benefits.

It proved difficult to resolve these differences when clinicians and health authorities weighed the considerations involved in treatment decisions independently of each other. On the other hand, when mechanisms were found to bring the two perspectives together, or to involve third parties, then the likelihood of finding common ground increased. The cases reported here include a variety of examples of how this was achieved with in some instances (for example Case 5) a compromise being reached and in others (for example Cases 2 and 3) the health authorities changing their decisions in the light of new evidence and independent advice. Only in two of the five cases did disagreement persist, with in Case 1 there being no room to compromise in what turned out to be an irreconcilable conflict between the family and the health authority, and in Case 4 the ruling of the High Court proving the decisive consideration. The health authority in Case 4 had attempted to bring the different parties together before the case went to court but in this instance it was not possible to reach agreement on what should be done.

In reflecting on these cases, it might be argued that in arriving at their initial decisions the health authorities gave insufficient consideration to values such as responsiveness to patients and respect for the autonomy of individuals. In fact, these were among the values considered by the health authority in Case 1, although they were not considered to be sufficiently important to outweigh the importance attached to equity and effectiveness. There is a direct parallel between this case and that of Child B, which illustrates the more general point made by Draper and Tunna in their discussion of the ethical dilemmas faced by NHS commissioners. As these authors note:

The process of commissioning is the process of adjudicating between the competing demands and needs of the local population. This process requires that each person is respected as an individual in his or her own right, that none is harmed by the services provided and that benefit for all is maximised. The conflict between the principles arises because there are insufficient funds to meet all needs as individuals prefer them to be met.

(Draper and Tunna, 1996, p.42)

Some health authorities have established committees to develop ethical frameworks to guide decision-making and to consider the principles of priority setting. In Oxfordshire a Priorities Forum brings together staff from the health authority, clinicians and others for this purpose. Their work has been developed with the support of an ethicist (Hope, Hicks, Reynolds, Crisp and Griffiths, 1998). This is a manifestation of a wider concern to strengthen the processes that underpin decision-making on priorities as a response to the ethical dilemmas involved in health care rationing. In the final chapter of this book we discuss this issue in more detail, both in relation to the role of health authorities and the responsibility that primary care groups will have in the future.

Chapter 4

Strengthening decision-making

A central conclusion of the Child B study was that the process of making decisions on priorities within the NHS should be strengthened. This conclusion was based on the view that these decisions are often controversial and contested, and achieving consensus between different actors is inherently difficult. It is therefore particularly important that the way in which decisions are reached is transparent and fair and helps to lend legitimacy to the choices that are made. How should this be done in a context in which demands outstrip the availability of resources and the commissioners of health services have to make difficult decisions on relative priorities?

Reason giving

Drawing on the research of Daniels and Sabin (1997) into priority setting in managed care organisations in the USA, the Child B study placed particular importance on 'reason giving' by health authorities in cases of the kind reported here. This included the opportunity for patients to appeal against decisions if they were dissatisfied with the outcome. As Daniels and Sabin argued, one of the effects of making public the reasons for decision would be to establish a body of 'case law' which:

> involves a form of institutional reflective equilibrium. The considered judgements reflected in past decisions constitute relatively fixed points that can be revised only with careful deliberation and good reasons. Overall, there is a commitment to coherence in the giving of reasons – decisions must fit with each other in a plausible reason- and principle-mediated way …

A commitment to the transparency that case law requires improves the quality of decision-making. An organisation whose practice requires it to articulate explicit reasons for its decisions becomes focused in its decision-making.

(Daniels and Sabin, 1997, pp.327–28)

In this paper and more recent writings, Daniels and Sabin set out four conditions, which they maintain would contribute to fairness and legitimacy in decision-making, and promote 'accountability for reasonableness'. These conditions are:

1 Publicity condition: Decisions regarding coverage for new technologies (and their limit-setting decisions) and their rationales must be publicly accessible

2 Relevance condition: These rationales must rest on evidence, reasons, and principles that all fair-minded parties (managers, clinicians, patients and consumers in general) can agree are relevant to deciding how to meet the diverse needs of a covered population under necessary resource constraints

3 Appeals condition: There is a mechanism for challenge and dispute resolution regarding limit-setting decisions, including the opportunity for revising decisions in light of further evidence or arguments

4 Enforcement condition: There is either voluntary or public regulation of the process to ensure that the first three conditions are met

(Daniels and Sabin, 1998, p.57)

Although developed in the context of decision-making by managed care organisations in the USA, the Child B study contended that these conditions were equally relevant to the NHS. In the case reported there, the Cambridge and Huntingdon Health Authority was found to have handled some aspects of decision-making well but in other respects there were ways in which it could have strengthened its approach and in the process secured greater understanding and support for its decision not to fund further intensive treatment for Jaymee Bowen. On this basis, the Child B study set out a series of proposals for how health authorities should approach priority setting in future. This is shown in the following box.

Health authorities need to:

- discuss and agree a set of values to guide decision-making, building on the values laid down by ministers, and involving other agencies such as NHS trusts. This includes debating what these values mean and testing them in both hypothetical and real cases

- clarify the process for making decisions on priorities, including arrangements for delegating responsibility from board level and for taking ECR decisions

- review arrangements for dealing with complex ECR decisions and for identifying and handling exceptions to agreed policies, including tertiary ECRs for which formal prior approval is no longer a standard requirement

- demonstrate that each case is examined on its merits taking into account all relevant facts

- ensure that the decision-making process is robust and enables relevant options to be examined rigorously

- obtain access to independent professional advice and draw up guidelines on how many professional views should be sought and the range of views that are relevant, especially when doctors disagree

- ensure that there is effective internal communication between those involved in decision-making

- provide patients with direct access to a designated decision-maker within the health authority in order to communicate the results of decisions effectively and to display appropriate sensitivity when difficult cases arise

- give reasons for decisions to fund or not fund treatment, explaining the basis of these decisions in order to demonstrate the legitimacy of the process, consistency and fairness

- establish an appeal mechanism to enable patients and their families to question and challenge decisions

- examine policies on communications and PR to ensure that effective arrangements are in place, should the need arise, for explaining the authority's position to the media and the public, including the roles to be played by different staff.

Source: Ham and Pickard (1998)

The evidence reported here reinforces the relevance of these proposals. The health authorities involved in the cases we have studied gave careful consideration to the choices with which they were confronted, including in some cases making use of values frameworks in arriving at decisions. They also called on independent advice when disagreements arose and tested out the options through internal debate and discussion. In one health authority a formal appeals procedure had been established, although this had fallen into disuse. The challenges launched by patients and families and the involvement of the courts were instrumental in forcing the health authorities to review their policies and procedures, and decision-making arrangements were strengthened as a consequence. Despite this, most of the authorities fell short of the approach proposed by Ham and Pickard (1998). Put another way, even after the Child B case, the NHS still lacks clear and consistent processes for making priority-setting decisions, and while the lessons learned from the experience reviewed here have been disseminated in part (as in Case 2 where regional public health networks were used for this purpose) practice continues to vary between districts.

Evidence

The argument can be taken a stage further by drawing on the work of Hadorn who identifies parallels between the health care system and the legal system, again in the context of the USA. Hadorn notes that decisions about health care have come to adopt some of the features associated with the legal system and he attributes this to 'The need to make relatively consistent case-by-case decisions amidst profound complexity' (Hadorn, 1992, p.83). He argues that decisions about health care, like legal decisions, should be based on formal consideration of the evidence about the outcome of care, and the formulation of judgements based on evidence. These judgements would be based on an explicit standard of proof, which might be more or less rigorous but would be required to demonstrate significant net health benefit before funding would be agreed. Hadorn acknowledges the complexities involved in this process and comments:

> *in the selection of a standard of proof … the fundamental balance between individual claims of need (that is, pursuit of individual good) and the greater public good is achieved* (p.93).

While Hadorn endorses the argument of Daniels and Sabin about the importance of due process in arriving at rationing decisions, he goes further by emphasising the need for decisions to be based on consideration of evidence of outcome. As such, his proposals speak to the wider debate about health care rationing, including the dispute between economists and policy analysts about the respective roles of evidence and processes in advancing this debate (Klein and Williams, 2000). The implication of Hadorn's work, and one we would share, is that evidence and processes both need to be strengthened. There are often disputes about the evidence on outcomes and how this should be interpreted. But developing decision-making processes is at least as important as carrying out more research into the effectiveness of different treatments in enabling rationing decisions to be seen to be fair and legitimate.

Primary care groups

In the next stage of development of the NHS, these arguments about decision-making processes apply as much to primary care groups as to health authorities in view of the responsibility placed on these groups to set priorities. The involvement of clinicians from primary care in these groups raises a further ethical dilemma in that it brings together in the same institution the individual and population perspectives on priority setting that, for the most part, have been separated until now. The question this raises is should clinicians act as agents for individual patients and for communities?

There are divergent views on this question with writers such as Sabin (1998) arguing that clinicians are particularly well positioned to assume both responsibilities and authors like Kassirer (1998) maintaining the opposite. Both authors contribute to this debate from a US perspective where the growth of managed care has led to a lively discussion about the ethical dilemmas facing clinicians and the potentially adverse impact on trust between patients and their doctors. The introduction of primary care groups and trusts into the NHS makes this discussion highly relevant to the UK.

Explicit decisions

This debate is in turn linked to discussion of whether it is desirable to make priority-setting decisions explicit at the micro level. The arguments of Daniels and Sabin (1998) are designed to encourage explicitness as part of the quest for greater accountability for reasonableness and as a contribution to enhanced democratic deliberation in health care. Mechanic (1997) takes a different view, drawing attention to the drawbacks of such an approach when much medical decision-making is surrounded by uncertainty and depends on clinical judgement. While there are strengths in Mechanic's position, the research we have reported here and elsewhere (Ham and Pickard, 1998) indicates the difficulties of relying on implicit decisions by clinicians. When doctors' expectations are rising and deference is declining, the demand for explicitness seems likely to grow as patients become more informed users and expect to have the basis of decisions that affect them or family members explained fully. This will not happen quickly – and some patients will continue to place their faith in doctors without seriously questioning their judgement – but in the long term we see little likelihood that medical paternalism and its attendant implicitness will survive in its traditional form.

Information and deliberation

How can we promote a more open approach that meets the expectations of patients and maintains trust in the doctor–patient relationship?

Informed choice

First, there is the provision of information to individual patients to enable them to assess the potential risks and benefits of alternative treatment options. This can be approached in a variety of ways including enabling access to the Internet and other sources and making available advice through the NHS. As recent research has shown, the quality of patient-based information is highly variable (Coulter, Entwistle and Gilbert, 1998) and if reliance is to be placed on this approach then controlling the quality of the advice offered is essential. Having made this point, making a reality of evidence-informed patient choice is beset with difficulties (Entwistle, Sheldon, Sowden and Watt, 1998) and it would be simplistic to assume that it can be implemented without confronting these difficulties openly.

Population level

Second, there is the debate about priority setting at a population level. The potential importance of the cases reported here is that in illustrating the difficulties of priority setting and the existence of 'tragic choices' in health care, they provide the basis for such a debate. Against this, the reluctance of politicians in the UK to lead such a debate and to continue to place the emphasis on local responsibility for decision-making means that public deliberation has not been taken forward except in a fragmented and ad hoc way. The establishment of the National Institute for Clinical Excellence offers the prospect of a more systematic discussion at a national level, although whether this occurs remains to be seen.

Trust

Maintaining trust in the doctor–patient relationship presents a different challenge given the risk that doctors will come to be seen as 'double agents' (Shortell, Waters, Clarke and Budetti, 1998) as they increasingly combine responsibilities for individual patients and populations. In this context, Mechanic's writings on trust are again worth noting as they suggest a variety of strategies that have been used. These strategies include:

● solicitation of consumer feedback

● informational programmes for patients and the public

● staff and professional education and sensitivity training

● sponsorship of support groups, patient empowerment programmes

● ethics consultation

● programmes to improve patient–professional relationships (Mechanic, 1996).

Mechanic's more recent papers elaborate on these initiatives and in the process testify to the efforts being made to address this challenge in the USA (Mechanic, 1998a; 1998b).

These issues have not received the same degree of attention in the UK but the implication of our research and of current policy developments indicates that they are likely to do so in future. Indeed, at a time when well-publicised failures of clinical performance have raised questions about standards of medical practice both in hospitals and primary care (Smith, 1998), the need to address the issue of trust is becoming increasingly urgent. To return to an earlier argument, primary care groups need to develop processes for making priority-setting decisions that enable them to demonstrate accountability for reasonableness and in so doing to maintain and strengthen trust between patients and doctors. At a minimum, this requires openness, reason-giving, an appeals procedure and regulation of the process to ensure that the conditions proposed by Daniels and Sabin (1998) are met. It also demands the use of evidence on effectiveness and agreement on the standard of proof required before the evidence is accepted as sufficient to support funding.

Conclusion

The research reported here both reinforces and modifies the conclusions of the Child B study. The most important conclusion is that those responsible for making contested decisions in health care need to adopt rigorous decision-making processes in order to demonstrate accountability for reasonableness to the populations served. The rise of consumerism and the increased willingness of patients and their families to use the courts to challenge decisions with which they disagree means that health authorities and primary care groups must show that they are handling each case on its merits and that they are consistent and fair in the way they discharge their responsibilities.

Health authorities and primary care groups also need to work closely with trusts and hospital clinicians in resolving contested decisions and seeking consensus. The advice of independent experts may assist in this process, particularly when there are differences between clinicians and patients on the one hand and the commissioners of care on the other. Contrary to the findings of the Child B study, our research indicates that direct communication between health authorities and patients will not always resolve the differences that give rise to contested decisions. This is not to argue that such communication should be avoided – rather, it is to urge caution in the quest for simple solutions to complex problems, and to underline the need for action on several fronts if the legitimacy of priority-setting decisions is to be ensured.

References

Academy of Royal Medical Colleges *et al. Priority Setting in the NHS: a discussion document.* London: Academy of Royal Medical Colleges, 1997.

Bowie C, Richardson A, Sykes W. Consulting the public about health service priorities. *BMJ* 1995; 311: 155–58.

Coulter A, Entwistle V, Gilbert D. *Informing Patients.* London: King's Fund, 1998.

Crisp R, Hope T, Ebbs D. The Asbury draft policy on ethical use of resources. *BMJ* 1996; 312: 1528–31.

Daniels N, Sabin J. Limits to Health Care: fair procedures, democratic deliberation and the legitimacy problem for insurers. *Philosophy and Public Affairs* 1997; 26: 303–50.

Daniels N, Sabin J. The ethics of accountability in managed care reform. *Health Affairs* 1998; 17: 50–64.

Draper H, Tunna K. *Ethics and Values for Commissioners.* Leeds: Nuffield Institute for Health, 1996.

Entwistle V, Sheldon T, Sowden A, Watt I. Evidence-informed patient choice. *International Journal of Technology Assessment in Health Care* 1998; 14: 212–25.

Hadorn D. Emerging parallels in the American health care and legal-judicial systems. *American Journal of Law and Medicine* 1992; 18: 73–96.

Ham C, Honigsbaum F, Thompson D. *Priority Setting for Health Gain.* London: Department of Health, 1993.

Ham C, Pickard S. *Tragic Choices in Health Care.* London: King's Fund, 1998.

Hope T, Hicks N, Reynolds D, Crisp R, Griffiths S. Rationing and the Health Authority. *BMJ* 1998; 317: 1067–69.

Kassirer JP. Managing care – should we adopt a new ethic? *NEJM* 1998; 339(6): 397–98.

Klein R, Day P, Redmayne S. *Managing Scarcity.* Buckingham: Open University Press, 1996.

Klein R, Williams A. Setting priorities: what is holding us back – inadequate information or inadequate institutions? In: Coulter A, Ham C, editors. *The Global Challenge of Health Care Rationing.* Buckingham: Open University Press, 2000.

Lenaghan J, New B, Mitchell E. Setting priorities: is there a role for citizens' juries? *BMJ* 1996; 312: 1591–93.

McIver S. *Healthy Debate? An independent evaluation of citizens' juries in health settings.* London: King's Fund, 1998.

Mechanic D. Changing medical organisation and the erosion of trust. *The Milbank Quarterly* 1996; 74(2): 171–89.

Mechanic D. Muddling through elegantly: finding the proper balance in rationing. *Health Affairs* 1997; 16(5): 83–92.

Mechanic D. Public trust and initiatives for new health care partnerships. *The Milbank Quarterly* 1998a; 76: 281–302.

Mechanic D. The functions and limitations of trust in the provision of medical care. *Journal of Health Politics, Policy and Law* 1998b; 23(4): 661–86.

Mooney G, Gerard K, Donaldson C, Farrar, S. *Priority Setting in Purchasing.* Birmingham: NAHAT, 1992.

Sabin J. Fairness as a problem of love and the heart: a clinician's perspective on priority setting. *BMJ* 1998; 317: 1002–04.

Shortell S, Waters T, Clarke KWB, Budetti PB. Physicians as double agents: maintaining trust in an era of multiple accountabilities. *JAMA* 1998; 280: 1102–08.

Smith R. All changed, changed utterly. *BMJ* 1998; 316: 1917–18.

Wall A. Every Manager's Nightmare. *Health Service Journal* 1995; 105: 24–26.